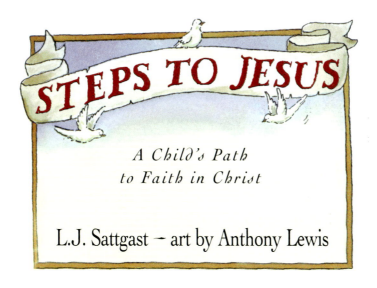

STEPS TO JESUS

A Child's Path
to Faith in Christ

L.J. Sattgast – art by Anthony Lewis

WATERBROOK
PRESS

STEPS TO JESUS

PUBLISHED BY WATERBROOK PRESS

5446 North Academy Boulevard, Suite 200

Colorado Springs, Colorado 80918

A division of Random House, Inc.

Scriptures in this book, unless otherwise noted, are from *New American Standard Bible* (NASB), copyright The Lockman Foundation, 1960, 1962, 1963, 1968, 1971, 1973, 1975, 1977. Used by permission, all rights reserved. Scripture quotations marked (TLB) are taken from *The Living Bible,* copyright © 1971. Used by permission of Tyndale House Publishers, Inc., Wheaton, Illinois 60189. Scripture quotations marked "NKJV" are taken from the *New King James Version.* Copyright © 1982 by Thomas Nelson, Inc. Scripture quotations marked (NCV) are taken from *The Holy Bible, New Century Version,* copyright © 1987, 1988, 1991 by Word Publishing, Nashville, TN 37214. All used by permission. All rights reserved.

ISBN 1-57856-190-6

LIBRARY OF CONGRESS CATALOGING-IN-PUBLICATION DATA

Sattgast, L. J., 1953-

    Steps to Jesus : a child's path to faith in Christ / L.J. Sattgast ; art by Anthony Lewis. — 1st ed.

    p. cm.

    Summary: Explains how God loves us, how disobeying God causes sadness, how Jesus came to save us from our sins, and how to grow as a child of God.

    ISBN: 1-57856-190-6

    1. Children—Religious life Juvenile literature. 2. Salvation Juvenile literature.

[1. Christian life. 2. Salvation.]

I. Lewis, Anthony, 1966- Ill. II. Title.

BV4571.2.S27   1999

248.8'2—dc21   99-26317

                                    CIP

Printed in the United States of America

1999—First Edition

10 9 8 7 6 5 4 3 2 1

Who Made the World?

Look around you.
What do you see?
Almost everywhere you go
there are people.
If you don't watch out,
you might bump into one of them!

There are girls and boys
and moms and dads
and aunts and uncles
and grandmas and grandpas.
Where did all these
people come from?

It was God who made people.
A long time ago
God made Adam and Eve,
the first man and woman.
They had children who grew up
and had children of their own.
Many years later, YOU were born.
YOU were made by God too.

People come in different shapes
and sizes and colors.
They may not dress like you
or speak your language,
but each person is special to God.
YOU are special to God too!

What else do you see
when you look around?
There are flowers to sniff,
tree branches to climb,
fat robins,
　　furry kittens,
　　　　playful puppies,
　　　　　　and other animals to love!

14

There are warm beaches
where you can make sand castles,
and ocean waves that invite you
to splash and jump.

There are frosty snowflakes
that tickle your nose
as you try to build
the biggest snowman in the world!

17

God made everything in this beautiful world.
He made it for you and for me
because He loves us.
He wants us to enjoy His world,
and He wants us to take care of it.

Basic Bible Truth:

God made us and gave us the earth to enjoy.
You can read about it in Genesis 1 and 2.

God made the sky
    and sea
    and land
    and all the plants.

God made the sun and moon and stars.

God made all the birds and fish and animals.

God made
    Adam and Eve
    and put them
    in charge of
    the new world
    He had made.

Why Are People Sad Sometimes?

Since God made us,
He knows what is best for us
and what will make us happy.
That is why He made some good rules
for us to follow.
We find God's good rules in the Bible.

The Bible tells us to love God
more than anything or anyone else.

The Bible tells us to love other people
and to treat them like we would want
to be treated.

The Bible tells us to obey our parents,
and it even tells our parents
how to be a good mom or dad.

In heaven, where God lives,
everyone obeys God's good rules.
But here on earth, where we live,
NO ONE has obeyed ALL of God's rules.
Even YOU have not obeyed all His rules.

That is why there is sadness
in God's beautiful world.
Disobeying God's good rules
is called sin, and sin makes people sad.

People sin when they fight
and call each other names.

People sin when they hit other people
and make them cry.

People sin when they steal things
that don't belong to them.

Sin does more than make us sad.
It makes us want to hide from God
and from other people.
If you have ever disobeyed your mom or dad,
you know what I mean.

But sin does something even worse.
It keeps us from being friends with God.
It means we can't belong to God's family
or go to heaven,
because sin is not allowed in heaven.

Basic Bible Truth:

Sin brings sadness into the world
and keeps us from being friends with God.
You can read about this in Genesis 3.

God told Adam and Eve
not to eat the fruit
from a certain tree.

Adam and Eve ate it anyway.

Adam and Eve tried to hide from God.

Adam and Eve were sad.
Now they could not
walk and talk with God
like they used to.

What Did God Do for Me?

God knew before He even made the world
that Adam and Eve would sin.
He knew that every person
born into the world from then on would sin.
He knew that even YOU
would disobey God's good rules.
So God already had a plan.

God sent His only Son, Jesus,
to be born into the world as a baby.
Jesus was different from everyone
who has ever been born.
He was perfect,
and He never sinned—
not even once.
He obeyed every one of God's good rules!

When Jesus was a young boy,
people noticed Him.
"What a good boy!" they said.
They did not know at first
that He was God's Son.

When Jesus grew up,
He began to do miracles.
Only God could do all the things
that Jesus did!
Jesus healed many sick people.

Jesus took five loaves of bread
and two small fish
and made so much food
that a big crowd of people
could not eat it all!
(Can you count how many baskets
were left over?)

Jesus told stories
to help explain God's good rules.
The people were amazed.
"We have never heard anyone teach
like this before," they said.

But then Jesus said something
that many of the people did not like.
"God is My Father," said Jesus.
"If you believe in Me and are sorry for your sins,
I will forgive you.
Then you can be part of His family
and go to heaven."

The leaders were angry with Jesus.
They did not believe
that Jesus was God's Son,
so they put Him on a cross to die.
"Forgive them, Father," said Jesus.
"They don't know what they're doing!"

Jesus did not deserve to die.
He had never done anything wrong.
But He let the leaders put Him on a cross.
He died and took our punishment
for breaking God's good rules.
His friends came and buried Jesus.
They thought that was the end.

But it was only the beginning.
Three days later
God raised Jesus from the dead.
Jesus was alive again!
Today Jesus still says to everyone,
"Believe in Me,
and I will wash your sins away.
You can become a child of God!"

BASIC BIBLE TRUTH:

Jesus took the punishment for our sins
so that we could become part of God's family.
You can read about it in John 3:16—

For God so loved the world,
that He gave His only begotten Son,
that whoever believes in Him
should not perish,
but have eternal life.

What Do I Have to Do?

When your parents give you a present,
you know that they love you.
They pick out something special,
and then they wrap it up for you.
The present probably cost them something.

But when they give you the present,
it really isn't yours
until you take it and unwrap it.
"Wow!" you say.
"It's just what I wanted! Thank you!"

God has a gift for you too.
It is the gift of salvation.
It means that God
will forgive all your sins.
The gift cost God a lot.
Jesus died so you could have this gift.
But the gift is not yours
until you choose to take it.

You can receive God's gift of salvation
right now.
Here's what you can tell God:

> Dear God, I'm sorry for my sins.
> I believe that Jesus is Your Son
> and that He died on the cross for me.
> Thank You for taking away my sins
> and for making me part of Your family!

When you pray
to receive God's gift of salvation,
it makes God and all the angels very happy!
You will be happy too.
You will probably want to tell
someone about it right away!

When you accept God's gift of salvation,
you become part of God's family.
Now you are called a Christian.
You belong to a big family
of people around the world
who are Christians too.

BASIC BIBLE TRUTH:

When you receive God's gift of salvation,
you become part of God's family.
You can read about it in John 1:12 and Luke 15:10—

But as many as received Him,
to them He gave the right
to become children of God,
even to those who believe in His name.

There is joy
in the presence of the angels of God
over one sinner who repents.

How Do I Grow as a Child of God?

Do you remember
when you were a baby?
Of course you don't!
That was so long ago,
and you have grown so much since then.
You grew tall and strong
because you ate good food and exercised.

When you become a child of God,
you are like a newborn baby.
All babies need to grow,
but how does a Christian grow?
Christians grow when they pray
and read the Bible,
and when they go to church to learn about God.

As you grow
you will learn more and more
about how much God loves you
and wants to help you follow His good rules.
Someday you will get to live in heaven with God,
but until then
you can talk to God any time you want
when you pray!

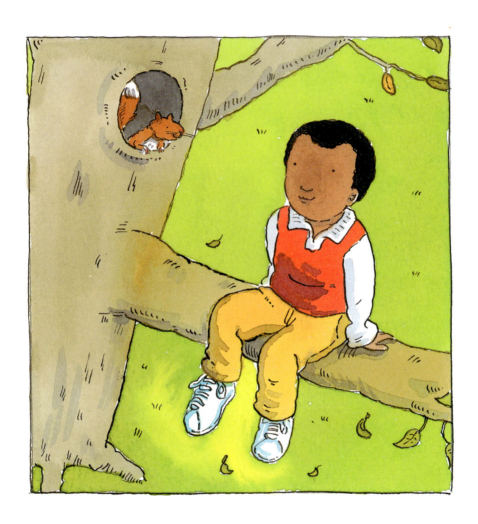

It's so great being a child of God!
You will want to tell other people
about Jesus and God's great gift of salvation,
for God wants everyone to join His family!

Basic Bible Truth:

God wants you to grow and become a strong Christian. You can read about it in 1 Peter 2:2, Hebrews 10:25, and 1 Peter 3:15—

As newborn babes, desire the pure milk of the word, that you may grow (NKJV).

You should not stay away
from the church meetings…
but you should meet together
and encourage each other (NCV).

If anybody asks
why you believe as you do,
be ready to tell him (TLB).

A NOTE TO PARENTS

It is a great joy and privilege to lead a child to Christ. If you have never done so, it is natural to have questions.

How old should my child be before I talk about salvation?
Read to your child from Bible storybooks at the earliest possible age, even before your child can talk or understand what you say. He or she will benefit from the comforting sound of your words and the intimate time you spend together. Little by little your child will begin to grasp the meaning of the words.

How do I know when my child is ready to make a decision about salvation?
Children as young as two or three have made meaningful decisions for Christ. Others do better if they are a little older. By spending time reading the Bible and praying with your child, you will know his or her level of *knowledge*. To find out the level of *understanding*, begin to ask questions such as these:

- Whom does God love?

- Why did Jesus come?

- What is sin?

Don't push for a decision before fully exploring how much your child understands. The younger the age, the more time and review is necessary. Remember, young children love repetition!

When your child knows the salvation basics and is able to understand that people need salvation, then you're ready for the next step.

How do I lead my child to Christ?
Now it's time to personalize the salvation story for your child. Watch for a tender heart-response to questions such as these:

- Have you sinned (disobeyed God)? *(yes)*

- When you sin, how does God feel? *(sad)*

- Can you go to heaven if you have sin in your heart? *(no)*

- Who can take away your sin? *(Jesus, God)*

- Would you like God (Jesus) to take away your sin? *(yes)*

If your child responds correctly to the preceding questions, he or she simply needs to be told (or reminded) that God is happy to take away our sins if we will just ask Him. Say a prayer out loud to demonstrate how this is done. You may use the prayer on page 74 if you wish.

Once you have demonstrated what needs to be done, ask if your child wants you to help him or her say the prayer, or if he or she wants to wait and think about it some more. More than likely, your child will say yes, but don't force a decision, even if you are sure your child understands.

What do I do next?

Give your child an opportunity to tell someone else about his or her decision.

- Make sure you and your child attend church regularly, but remember that, ultimately, it is your God-given privilege and responsibility to help your child grow spiritually.

- Model the Christian walk for your child.

- Pray for your child regularly.

- Make sure your child understands the following principles:

—Once we become a child of God, we don't need to pray for salvation again and again, or worry about losing our salvation. (John 1:12-13; Ephesians 1)

—We do, however, need to learn how to confess our sins so we can live in harmony with God and others. (1 John 1:9)

Will my child forget that he or she prayed to receive salvation?

If your child is very young it is possible that he or she will forget. Fill out the salvation "certificate" on the following page and display it somewhere in your home or your child's room. Talk about it once in a while or ask questions now and then to make sure your child still understands what salvation means.

A child who doesn't remember may want to pray again "just to be sure" when he or she is older, perhaps in grade school or at camp. This is perfectly natural and does not mean that the original prayer was ineffective. There will be points all along your child's journey with Jesus at which a deeper commitment to follow Christ will be a necessary part of his or her Christian growth.

SALVATION CERTIFICATE:

I, _____ ,

NAME OF CHILD

asked Jesus to forgive my sins
and make me part of His family on

_____

DATE

_____

WITNESS

Now I Am a Child of God!